INTRODUCTION

Imagine that your mother is a quantum electronics researcher with an experimental lab in your basement, and she leaves the key to the lab in a really obvious spot. You might want to sneak down to the lab at night and start playing around with the equipment. You might learn a massive amount about experimental electronics. You might even make a radical discovery while you are messing around with the programming code of your favourite game, VR technology and some nifty quantum electro-tube gizmos. A radical discovery that lets you and your two best friends enter right into your favourite game. I don't have to imagine, because I'm Duncan and this is exactly what happened to me.

MEET THE GLITCH FORCE

DUNCAN

A genius redstoner who can't resist testing out the quantum electronic gizmos in his mother's research lab.

MIRANDA

A sharpshooter with encyclopedic knowledge of Minecraft.

ZED

An expert builder with a prankster heart.

Chapter 1: Anomaly

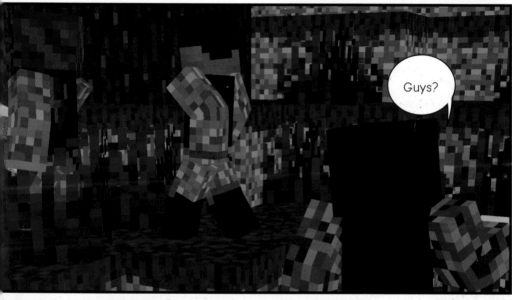

These things are everywhere!

Look – there's a house! let's go in.

Phew.

Um. I'm not sure this was the best choice.

We're in a woodland mansion...

...home of the evoker.

CHAPTER 2:
EVOKER

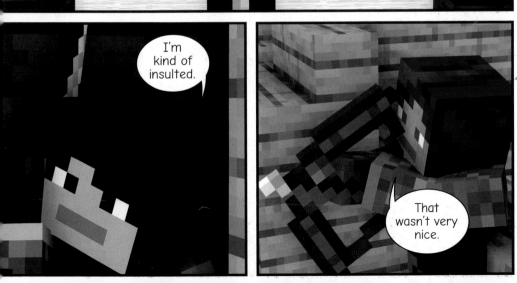

CHAPTER 3:
WOOL

All clear – let's go!

Now which way?

These mansions are randomly generated, so the next stairs could be in either direction.

Let's go this way.

We have to keep pushing forward.

Let's go room by room and keep out of the corridors as much as possible.

There's a room up here.

Weird. It's some kind of map room. Let's keep going.

Another room coming up.

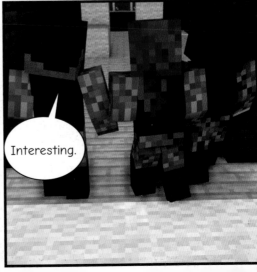

Interesting.

Chapter 4:
Loot

Nope! Not this one either.

Nope, but that's creepy.

Nope!

Bingo! Loft bedroom.

I bet there's a chest in the loft.

Holy Moley!

String, please. I can make a bow.

Take it all and let's keep going!

Here, have a diamond sword! And an axe! And string! And an iron bucket.

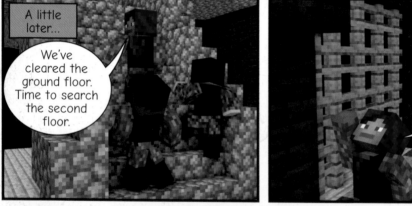

A little later...

We've cleared the ground floor. Time to search the second floor.

Here's another loot room. The che is up there, above the door.

Another diamond sword and a golden apple. Redstone dust. An enchanted bow. So much stuff!

Take it all.

We've scoured both floors without runnin into one illager Let's go to the third floor. We passed the sta room a little while back.

We can get through this window here.

CRACK!

CRACK!

This is crazy. We're on the roof of a woodland mansion in the middle of the dark forest, in Minecraft!

It feels like we've been in Minecraft forever.

Can you believe we were in Duncan's room, staring at his crazy contraption, just this morning?

CHAPTER 5:
BACK TO THE
BEGINNING

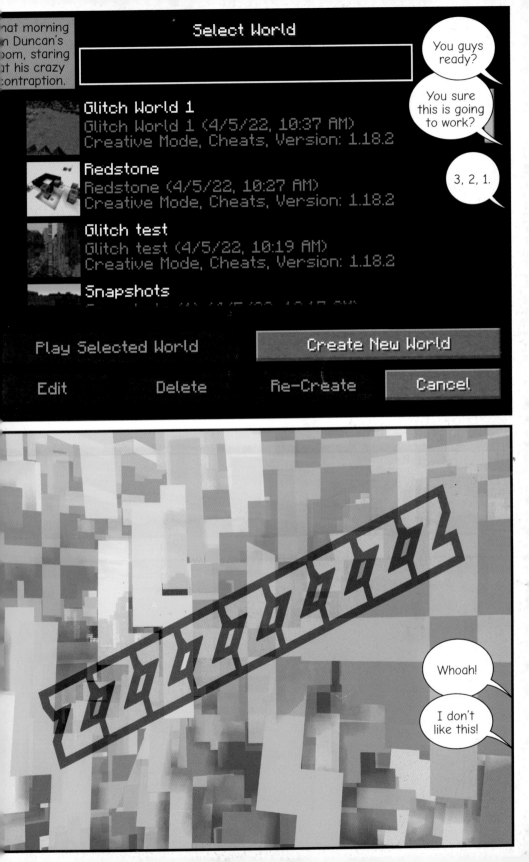

Whooo!

I'm so fast!

And now I'm not. I can't run anymore.

We forgot food.

We need to kill sheep for wool to make beds and then eat the mutton.

Look. There are sheep over there.

I don't know about this. Maybe we can find some potatoes?

It's okay. They're just made of pixels. They're not real sheep. Even if it feels real, we're like... it's like Virtual Reality.

VR. Right.

It's huge.

No time to waste.

Okay, we need to steer clear of the powder snow. It's a little bluer than the nice snow, so keep an eye out. Let's go to that rocky area.

Hey, there's a ton of iron up here.

And coal.

A few minutes later...

OK, I've got a bunch of iron.

Me too. I should build the return glitch contraption right here. We still need to get redstone, but I can start with what I have.

CHAPTER 6:
HESS

Well, we've had reports of six glitches so far, and they seem to be causing problems.

Six? I don't understand. That's not possible. We only created one glitch.

There was a glitch by my village and I'll tell you it's making some people very unhappy.

How did you link it to us?

When someone in my village reported seeing another glitch out on the plains, I came to look around. I found where you had lunch and where you destroyed that zombie. I saw you go up the mountain, so I followed you.

Can you show us what has everyone upset?

How far is your village?

Not far. Follow me.

veral minutes later.

Ve got stuff!

I think that's it.

Okay, stand ack. I'm going to ip this switch and he reverse glitch pefully should do the trick.

CLICK!

ZZZZZZ!

No more potatoes!

Ban Free Potatoes

No Free Potato

Hurray!

Ooooh. Campfire signals. Like Morse code communication from other villages.

Yeah, smoke signals. We can create plumes of different sized smoke blobs in a special order and it's like sending a coded message. Any villager who can see the smoke plumes and knows the code can read it.

So we know the general areas where we saw the smoke signals, but that's it.

Hmm. I think I can make a glitch sensor to detect where a new glitch has occurred. It will need to be constructed somewhere in the nearby vicinity of the glitch.

Why?

The sensor needs to be placed close to quantum traces of the glitch in order to detect them.

To get to the general area, I think I can modify my original glitch contraption.

I'm going to need some more supplies. And we need to go back up the mountain.

Follow me.

Just give me a couple minutes here.

What else did you bring for supplies, besides the delicious carrots?

Here's an iron sword, a bow, arrows and a diamond axe. Plus more redstone stuff.

Now, tell me where a glitch was and let me calibrate.

It was about five biomes away, to the west, in a dark forest.

CHAPTER 7:
GRAVEL

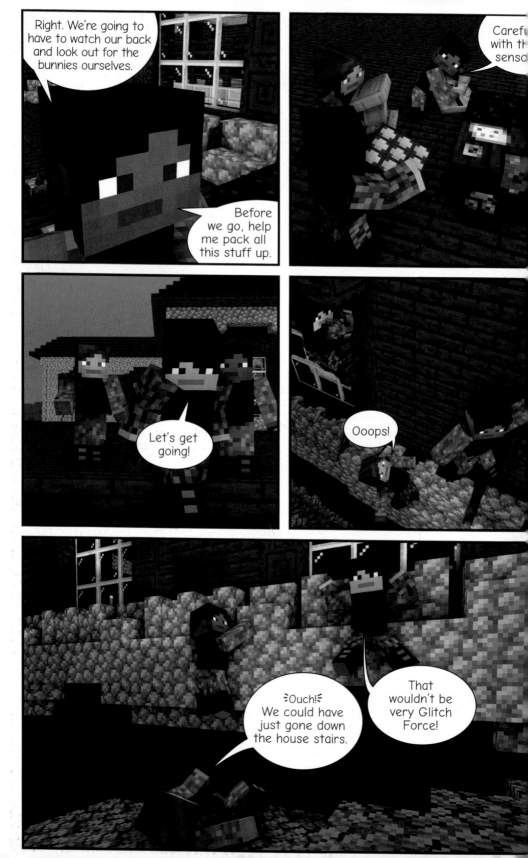

No, just send them back to wherever they came from. Like the potatoes.

If it's an energy imbalance th[at] caused this problem, we need t[o] send about the same amount o[f] energy and mass that came i[n] through the glitch out o[f] the glitch.

Look. Gravel.

So what?

I want to get some flint so we can have a flint and steel. It's a good tool to have in our arsenal for making fire or lighting a portal or setting enemies on fire, or whatever. Plus, I need it if I need to make more arrows.

Good idea. We should all have a flint and steel.

Hold on. The gravel is collapsing!

FsFsFsSfS

What on earth just happened?

Gravel. It can generate above air, and it stays in place until you touch it, and then it drops.

WHIZZ!

Watch out! Nearby hostile activity detected!

Made it!

Well, that was a fun detour. We got in some caving, some mining, some looting and some fighting!

Ooof.

Could you be just a little less cheery, Zed?

So I'm guessing you guys are tired.

What gave it away?

CHAPTER 8:
HUNGRY

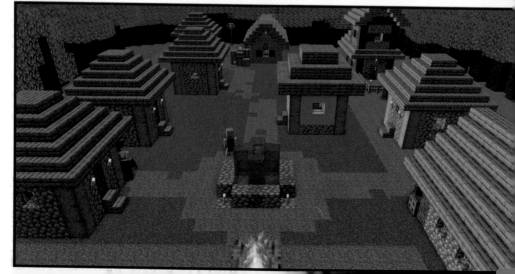

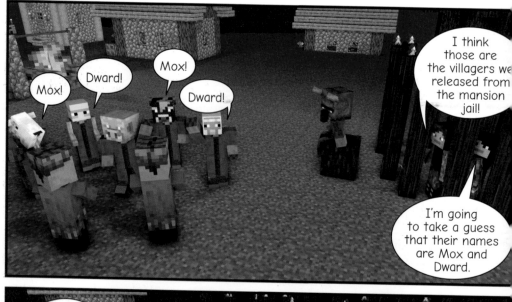

In a pit. He mad.

Come.

Len is the guy that thought we'd make good starters.

I don't think he's changed his mind.

Aarrrrgh!

How about this. We can cure him. We have all the ingredients with us.

If we cure him, will you let us go free?

CHAPTER 9:

HUNT

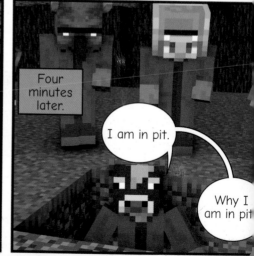

A massive rabbit's foot!

So... why did you make a hidden village in the dark forest?

We all escaped from the mansion. One or two at a time. And built our village to help other escapees. Baaa.

So the illagers captured you and took you to the mansion?

Baaa. Yes. Bring us villagers there and then give us animal heads and stuff. Well, you see. Evil they are.

Well, we've got good news for you.

We've killed all the illagers in the mansion. It's illager-free!

That didn't get the response I wanted.

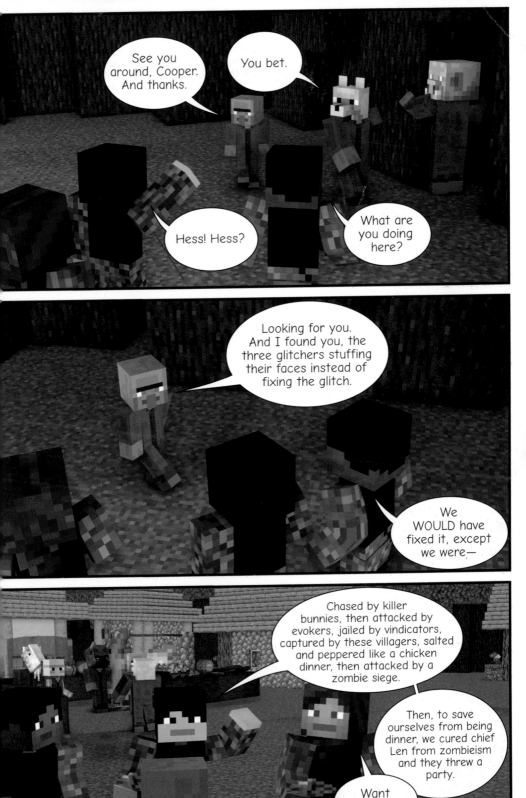

Sure. I didn't hear anything from you for over a day. So I decided to follow you and see what's what.

How'd you follow us?

I used your little glitch contraption.

What?

I watched you. Step in and press the button.

Okay.... I'm not sure that was a great idea, but....

So did you find out what the glitch was?

Giant rabbits' feet?

A little later.

Drat! It's off again.

It went into the hole. Looks like that other hole we saw.

What is that? Is that another glitch?

It's a warren. A giant killer bunny warren.

So they're hiding down there?

They're nesting.

Nesting?

Making more giant killer bunnies.

Chapter 10: Warren

ZING!

BONK!

I hit it, but it's not stopping!

Quick! Let's follow!

It's taking Hess back to the warren!

We've got to go in.

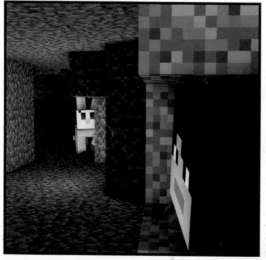

I'll mark this spot on our map. We get out of here, and dig straight down to Hess. Someone's going to have to rope down and grab him. Then we pull him up, straight outta the warren.

The bunnies will go crazy.

Not if they're sleeping.

We can hope.

I have a lead I got from one of the mansion loot chests. You let me down on a rope, and I'll use the lead to grab Hess.

If we can get up to the canopy fast, and use the rabbit skins to mask our smell, we should be able to get away.

CHAPTER 11:
EXTREMES

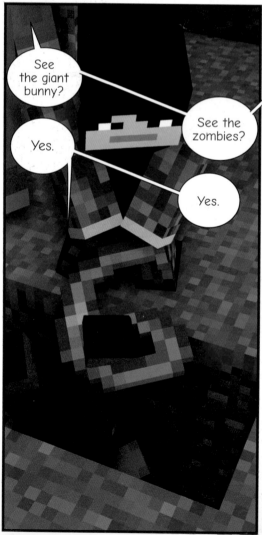

Oh, bunnies...

You bad evil bunnies...

It's tasty Zed, strolling around in your warren.

ᶠEeeee!ᶠ

ᶠEeeeeee!ᶠ

ᶠEeeeee!ᶠ

They're coming!

ᶠEeeeee!ᶠ

ᶠEee!ᶠ

ᶠEEEEᶠ

ᶠEeeee!ᶠ

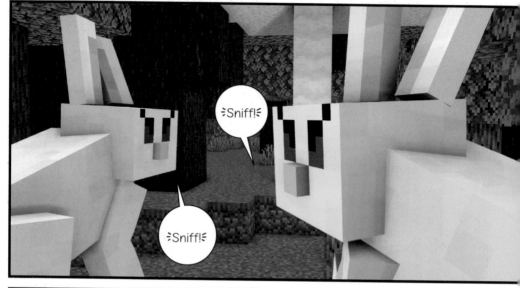

Chapter 12:
Bonfire